ESSENTIAL TIPS

Planning a
SMALL GARDEN

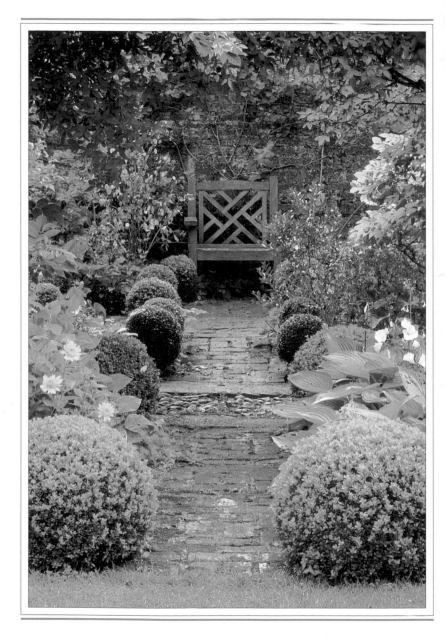

Planning a
SMALL GARDEN

CONTRIBUTING EDITOR
John Brookes

DORLING KINDERSLEY
London • New York • Stuttgart • Moscow

A DORLING KINDERSLEY BOOK

Editor Damien Moore
Art Editor Alyson Kyles
DTP Designer Mark Bracey
Series Editor Charlotte Davies
Series Art Editor Clive Hayball
Production Controller Lauren Britton

First published in Great Britain in 1996 by
Dorling Kindersley Limited,
9 Henrietta Street, London WC2E 8PS
Reprinted 1996

A CIP catalogue record for this book is available from the British Library

ISBN 07513-0279-1

Text film output by The Right Type, Great Britain
Reproduced by Colourscan, Singapore
Printed and bound by Graphicom, Italy

ESSENTIAL TIPS

PAGES 38-42

CONSIDERING SURFACES

PAGES 43-47

PLANNING YOUR PLANTING

PAGES 48-51

PLANTING ENVIRONMENTS

BASIC DESIGN CONSIDERATIONS

1 MAKING THE MOST OF YOUR SPACE

To realize the potential of a small space you must firstly abandon your preconceptions about the nature of a "garden" – the word often evokes visions of lawns and flowerbeds. Traditional planting is, however, only one of the options open to you.

Any outdoor space, be it a rooftop, a basement site, or a window ledge, can be treated as a "garden" in that, with a little careful planning and a practical design, the most neglected space can be converted into an attractive extension of your home.

△ SUSPENDED SPLENDOUR
*A hanging basket provides a
versatile option for small-
scale gardening. Here, the
pelargoniums and verbenas
ensure long-term colour.*

△ VERTICAL PLANTING
*A bare wall is transformed
by a spectacular display of
climbing and trailing plants.*

◁ CONTAINER GARDENING
*Use containers to introduce
colour and fragrance into
awkward locations such as
rooftops or basements, which
are impossible to garden in
the traditional sense.*

2 AN OUTDOOR ROOM

Think of your outside space as a "room"
where you can eat, entertain guests, or enjoy a
moment of solitude away from the pressures of
urban living. Although this is easier to imagine
in a Mediterranean climate, sun alone does not
make for a comfortable outdoor space. Consider
how you can minimize draughts, create a degree
of privacy, disguise ugly views, and use colour
and fragrance to create a pleasing ambience.

A GARDEN SANCTUARY

3 FOUR KEY FACTORS

It is worth investing plenty of time at the
planning stage of designing your garden. You
must try to find a design that satisfies a number
of variable factors: the way you wish to use the
space, the limitations of the site, the character
of the surroundings, and the amount of money
available for materials and plants.

4 INSIDE-OUT GARDENING

Make sure that your outdoor space is attractive when viewed from inside. A cramped garden will seem less so if it is a harmonious extension of the interior room that it adjoins.
- Analyze your interior design: is it period or modern? Consider how you can interpret the style outdoors.

- Consider how you can harmonize colour in your house and garden.
- If possible, choose the same type of flooring for your garden space as you have used for your inside space.
- Choose furniture that is suitable for outdoor or indoor use to extend the link between the two spaces.

5 COMPLEMENTARY ELEMENTS

In order to create a coherent and pleasing style in your outside space, you must treat each element of your garden – be it walls, fences, furniture, steps, or plant pots – as part of a single design. Bear in mind how one relates to another in terms of colour, shape, and texture, as well as function. A piecemeal approach – building a raised bed here, planting a shrub there – and an assortment of ill-considered bits and pieces will result in an unstylish mishmash, and will also make your small space seem even smaller than it actually is. A successful garden, whether it be at ground level or on a balcony or rooftop, is one in which all its elements, from the smallest to the biggest, are in accord.

◁ GOTHIC-STYLE GARDEN
This individual creation may not be to everyone's taste, but it is certainly a bold design that makes a positive and coherent statement visually.

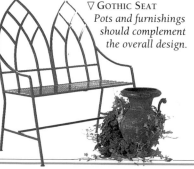

▽ GOTHIC SEAT
Pots and furnishings should complement the overall design.

6 FIND YOUR OWN STYLE

Plan your own garden to satisfy yourself and your family and not necessarily other people. Wholesale copying of another design may result in disappointment. It is, of course, a good idea to study other people's designs (and various national styles) as sources of inspiration. But ultimately you must seek to evolve a style that suits your personality, because your garden, like your clothes or your furnishings, should be an expression of your own taste. Adopt a design that suits your lifestyle. For example, you must consider whether you have the time or, indeed, the inclination to nurture plants, or would you need or prefer a low-maintenance garden?

△ NATIONAL STYLES
Seek inspiration from the simplicity of an oriental-style design (see p.68).

△ FORMAL GARDEN
Formal garden styles such as this require regular and meticulous maintenance.

▽ PERIOD OR MODERN?
These garden accessories would be suitable only in a modern-style garden.

△ LOW-MAINTENANCE GARDEN
A garden where the textures and colours of the structure take precedence over the planting is suitable if your busy lifestyle leaves little time for gardening.

7 ARCHITECTURAL REFLECTIONS

It is likely that the style of your home has already influenced your choice of interior decorations and furnishings. Let it do the same for your garden. Each architectural style has facets that can be reflected in the line and form of the garden's layout, whatever its size.

■ Select materials that complement those from which your house is made: stone, brick, or timber.

■ Select and arrange containers and furnishings – and even plants – that reflect the style of your house.
■ You do not have to be historically accurate in every detail, but try to capture the general mood of a style.

▽ REFLECTIONS IN WINDOWS
Here, flint cobbles surrounding a young fig tree echo the materials used in the walls of the house. The mass of planting reflects the rural style of the building.

SPECIFIC SITES

8 WINDOWS

Choose plants and containers that suit the style of your window by looking at the colour of the window frame and its surround.

■ If you have no window sill or your window opens outwards, hang pots beneath your window or grow a climber from ground level and train it around the frame.

DELICATE DISPLAY ▷
A vine, Vitis, *and a window-box planted with delicate pelargoniums decorate this simple window and its rustic surround.*

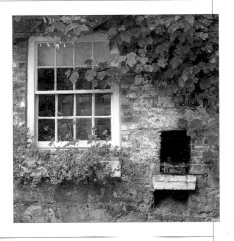

9 BALCONIES

Balconies are often buffeted by strong winds, so select plants that will thrive in exposed conditions (*see p.51*). Grow less hardy species in the shelter of the hardier plants. Train climbers like ivy up a secured trellis to give shelter and a measure of privacy, or to obscure an ugly view. Make sure you secure any containers and furnishings so they do not to present a danger to your neighbours below.

◁ HEAVYWEIGHT CONTAINERS
Pots of plants, especially when wet, can be very heavy. Consult a structural engineer about the weight capacity of your balcony.

10 CREATING A ROOFTOP RETREAT

As far as possible, treat your roof space as you would an indoor space, so that you create a room-like atmosphere. Weather-proof flooring or lightweight paving will make your roof-space more congenial. Be sure to consult a structural engineer to establish the strength of your roof.

■ It is advisable to choose lightweight pots for plants, and to place them close to supporting walls.

LIGHTWEIGHT CONTAINER ▷
A lightweight wooden window-box is a practical option for most roof sites.

▽ STURDY SITUATION
This rooftop site is sturdy enough to support a veritable forest of shrubs and trees, including juniper and New Zealand flax in heavy terracotta pots.

■ Choose and arrange your planting carefully – many species will not tolerate exposure to intense rooftop sunshine and strong wind (*see p.51*).
■ Spread a layer of gravel or pebbles over the surface of soil in pots. This will help retain moisture and stop the top surface from blowing away.

11 HOW TO ENHANCE A BASEMENT SITE

Low areas such as basements can be gloomy and damp. However, there are many ways of making such areas stylish and pleasant to use.

- Repair or, if necessary, install a damp-proof course to ensure garden moisture does not infiltrate indoors.
- Experiment with colour to bring interest to a basement area and to brighten it up if it is shady. Consider painting the walls or laying bright or colourful surfacing materials.

- Mirrors can make your site seem larger and increase light for plants.
- Provide a feature, whether a piece of sculpture, a seat, or a plant, to anchor the eye within the site.
- Choose plants that are tolerant of shade (see p.50), many of which have interesting foliage shapes.
- Create single-colour planting schemes, in light tones of gold and silver, as an effective way of bringing life to a shady basement area.

◁ A MOSSY POT
A water feature anchors the eye within this shady site.

▽ SHADE-LOVING PLANT
This elegant Solomon's seal, Polygonatum, *with forget-me-nots,* Myosotis, *will thrive in the shade.*

12 HOW TO ENHANCE NARROW SPACES

Build up an internal structure that draws the eye from side to side to create an impression of breadth in a narrow space, and use screens to break up the view down the garden. Screens can also block draughts – a common problem in narrow sites.

Long narrow spaces draw the eye through them – a disadvantage if the end point is a dilapidated fence. Turn this into a positive quality by placing a dramatic feature, such as a statue, a large urn, or a *trompe l'oeil*, at the bottom of the garden.

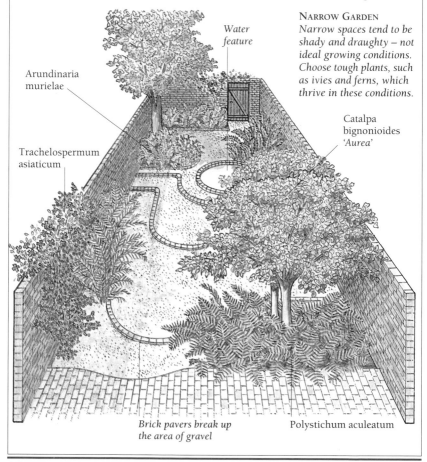

NARROW GARDEN
Narrow spaces tend to be shady and draughty – not ideal growing conditions. Choose tough plants, such as ivies and ferns, which thrive in these conditions.

Water feature

Arundinaria murielae

Trachelospermum asiaticum

Catalpa bignonioides 'Aurea'

Brick pavers break up the area of gravel

Polystichum aculeatum

13 DECORATIVE DOORWAYS

The material you select for surfacing around your doorway, the style and colour of your door, its fixtures and fittings, and pots and tubs placed around it should all suit the style of your home and set the mood for what lies within. Choose a light, or a pot for the doorway, or hang a garland on the door to make your entrance welcoming to visitors. But be sure that such items are firmly attached, for weight alone is no deterrent to a determined thief.

◁ COUNTRY-STYLE ENTRANCE
This porch was added to the cottage by its new owners, but it is designed in keeping with the older building.

14 IMAGINATIVE STEPS

Steps afford the frustrated urban gardener valuable space for growing plants (in pots alongside the steps or on the steps themselves).
■ Plants alongside steps should have bold, architectural shape to balance the strong structural form of the steps themseves. Evergreen shrubs are ideal, as they give year-round shape and interest to your planting.
■ Select climbing plants to decorate hand-rails and adjacent walls.
■ Grow colourful annuals in pots on the steps themselves – but do not impede the pathway.

△ LEAVING SPACE FOR THYME
These attractive garden steps have been designed to include planting space for a mat-forming plant such as this thyme.

BOUNDARY STRUCTURES

15 WALLED GARDENS

In urban areas, small gardens are often hemmed in by the walls of neighbouring gardens or buildings. The effect is often constricting, but the following measures can help:

■ Grow climbing plants to bring life and colour to ugly, oppressive walls.

■ Use retaining walls within your garden to add interest and to lead the eye from the top of the boundary wall down to ground level.

■ Include bold internal features, such as a mass of planting or a statue, to hold the eye within the site.

△ A RURAL SETTING
This stone wall, although an attractive feature in itself, also provides a splendid foil for this elegant, winding wisteria.

16 DECORATING WALLS

Do not be afraid to decorate your outside wall in a similar manner to walls in your house.
- Painting walls will enliven a small enclosed space and counteract its oppressiveness.
- Attach shelves to your walls to support pots and curiosities such as exotic shells and pebbles.
- Decorate exterior walls with sculptural panels, plaques, and tiles, just as you would indoors.
- Use planted trelliswork to disguise ugly walls.

△ WALL FLOWER
Clematis is a very popular twining plant, renowned for its long flowering period.

▽ A SOFT OPTION
A mass of planting softens the hard line of the wall.

△ FERNS & FLOWERS
Here, a courtyard wall is decorated with trelliswork hung with an array of pots and plants, including many ferns that thrive in shade.

◁ CERAMIC SUNSHINE
A ceramic sun creates a simple and charming focal point on an outdoor wall.

17 WALL FLOWERS

In gardens where ground space is limited climbing plants are invaluable, but they bring an effective vertical element to any garden design.

- Evergreen climbers, such as the passion flower (*Passiflora caerulea*) shown below, are especially useful because they provide a strong structural element in the garden all year round.
- Clothing a wall with a combination of climbers can bring continual interest. Clematis and vines are especially happy to grow through other plants.
- If you do not have a suitable wall or fence on which to grow climbing plants, you can make or purchase a free-standing support in trellis or cane.

◁ PASSION FLOWER

FAVOURITE CLIMBERS
Actinidia chinensis
Akebia quinata
Berberidopsis corallina
Campsis grandiflora
Clematis alpina
Clematis montana
Clianthus puniceus
Hedera colchica
Hedera helix hibernica
Humulus lupulus
Ipomoea hederacea
Jasminum mesnyi
Jasminum officinale
Lonicera japonica
Lonicera periclymenum
Passiflora caerulea
Polygonum baldschuanicum
Vitis coignetiae
Vitis vinifera
Wisteria sinensis

△ TRAINING SHRUBS
Some shrubs, such as this evergreen Ceanothus, *can be trained to climb up walls.*

◁ CLIMBING ROSES
This brick and stone wall is a handsome feature in its own right. It is an ideal foil for the elegant climbing rose in this unruly, country-style garden.

18 MATERIALS FOR WALLS

When choosing material for a wall, consider how the colour and texture will complement your house and its surrounding structural elements.

■ Always take into consideration the unit size of different materials.

■ Visualize the massed effect of a unit – it can be startlingly different to looking at a unit in isolation.

■ Brick is the most popular material for building walls. The enormous range available means that there is a brick to suit almost any setting.

■ In rural locations, local stone will probably best suit the landscape; in urban areas, concrete is often better.

△ MIXED MATERIALS
Using a combination of building materials can be highly effective. This striking wall was constructed with a mixture of brick and flint – ideal for this country garden.

◁ CONCRETE BRICK
These small-scale rock-faced concrete blocks are designed to imitate the effect of traditional clay bricks.

△ PRE-CAST BLOCKS
These sandstone coloured concrete blocks contain a medium-textured aggregate.

MOTTLED BRICKS △
With a rough-hewn appearance, these engineering bricks are the hardest of all traditional bricks.

△ GEOMETRIC PATTERNS
Although much maligned, this modern type of concrete block is relatively cheap, and it is easier to erect than traditional brick.

NATURAL STONES ▷
Dry-stone walls are lovely features. The crevices between the stones are ideal for many rock plants.

NATURAL
LIMESTONE

NATURAL
SANDSTONE

19 FENCING FOR YOUR BOUNDARIES

Fencing is a highly versatile and relatively inexpensive material for marking the boundaries of your site. Fences are easier to erect than walls and make good backdrops for planting, but they do require more maintenance. The fact that fences provide almost instant privacy gives them an advantage over hedging.

■ Use high panels of solid fencing to create a wall-like barrier that is relatively easy to erect. Remember, however, that this type of boundary can make your small site feel even smaller and rather claustrophobic.
■ See-through fencing at any height makes a small space feel larger and is an ideal host for climbing plants.

△ TRADITIONAL PICKET FENCING
This garden is enclosed by a traditional white picket fence, which complements the cottage's attractive whitewashed walls.

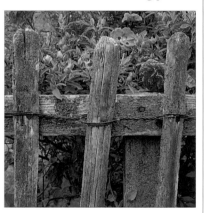

△ PLANTING THROUGH FENCING
Shrub roses and cistus have been planted alongside this old, weathered fence to create a traditional rustic feel.

20 BORROW YOUR NEIGHBOUR'S GARDEN

When you are dividing your small plot of land from that of your neighbours, consider the advantage of visually sharing the space. Even a small panel of open fencing will help counteract the boxed-in feeling that can be created by solid fencing.

Open-style fencing will enable you to enjoy the plants growing on your neighbour's side of the fence as well as your own. But bear in mind the possibility that if your neighbour's garden is neglected you may inherit just invasive weeds and an eyesore.

21 CHOOSING BOUNDARY FENCING

As with other structural features, care must be taken when selecting a fence to complement the style of your house. You must also consider practical matters, such as the privacy and shelter afforded.

- Wood is the most popular material for fences, and there is a style of timber fencing to suit almost any purpose and every location.

- It is generally a false economy to invest in too cheap a fence. Inferior material will deteriorate rapidly.
- Remember that timber rots if left in direct contact with the ground, so verticals should be placed in a metal shoe and set in concrete.
- Metal and plastic are alternative fencing materials, which need less maintenance than timber.

RUSTIC WEAVES ▷
Country-style woven and lattice-work fences can be extremely attractive in the right location. However, the lifespan of such fences is limited.

WILLOW HURDLES ▷

HAZEL HURDLES ▷

SOFTWOOD LATTICE ▷

△ PANEL FENCING
This type of fencing is composed of horizontal softwood slats. Allowing maximum privacy, it is ideal for urban areas.

△ BAMBOO
Bamboo lengths, which are an ideal choice for an oriental-style garden (see p.68), can be bound together to make a solid or openwork fence.

△ CLOSEBOARD
This type of fencing is constructed by nailing feather-edged verticals to horizontal rails.

△ PICKET FENCING
Highly decorative, picket fencing allows passers-by enjoyment of your garden.

22 HEDGES

Consider using hedging as an attractive alternative to a boundary wall or fence. Hedging provides a dramatic backdrop for planting, and can also make a strong and colourful feature in its own right. However, as hedging absorbs nutrients out of the soil, it may not be a good choice if your borders are narrow or your soil is particularly dry.

SETTING THE STAGE ▷
This neatly trimmed yew hedge makes a tall, dramatic backdrop for a stunning mass of purple lavender.

23 CHOOSING A BOUNDARY HEDGE

When selecting a hedge, first consider what its function will be. If your first priority is privacy, then an evergreen hedge, such as yew or box, which does not shed its leaves in winter, is the best choice.

Consider, too, the potential height of your hedge planting. Some of the plants that are selected for hedges grow naturally into forest trees. Plants with berries, such as holly, can make attractive hedges.

YEW
As an evergreen hedge, Taxus baccata *provides year-round interest.*

BOX
A dense evergreen, Buxus sempervirens *is ideal for creating a sculptural effect.*

LAUREL
Prunus laurocerasus *makes a tall, attractive hedge with its shiny evergreen foliage.*

24 DEFENSIVE GARDENING

Deter prowlers and other unwelcome individuals by planting a boundary hedging of shrubs with spines or thorns, such as berberis, or ones with spiky leaves, such as holly, *Ilex*. These plants are often handsome as well as extremely vicious, so they present the security-conscious householder with a more aesthetically pleasing option than the various man-made deterrents, such as barbed wire.

△ HOLLY, *ILEX* SP.

BEECH
Fagus sylvatica, *a deciduous species, will naturally grow over 6m (20ft) tall.*

△ FIRETHORN
This window is protected by the viciously spiny branches of firethorn, Pyracantha, *which has clusters of white flowers in summer.*

HOLLY, *ILEX AQUIFOLIUM* 'GOLDEN QUEEN'

INTERNAL FEATURES

25 THE IMPORTANCE OF STRUCTURAL STYLE

The structure of your garden can be an exciting feature in its own right, and may well need to be if, as is often the case, its size and location allows little or no scope for planting. Even for those with more space, the structure is important, for a mass of plants will become a nondescript mess if it is not contained and offset by a strong permanent structure.

- The materials used to construct the garden, the way they are arranged, and the style of furnishings (which include pots, sculptural features, and lighting), all mould its character.
- As well as looking at the practical pros and cons of different materials and structural styles, consider how you can integrate "inherited" (often unwelcome) features into the design.

△ PERGOLAS, PLANTS, & POTS
A pergola defines a paved terrace area, which is a perfect place to sit and enjoy the garden or entertain friends. These strong structural elements are balanced by a mass of planting.

△ SMALL DETAILS
Minor elements in your garden, such as edging stones, should still integrate with major ones.

◁ FOCAL POINT
A piece of sculpture can act as a visual punctuation mark in a small garden design.

26 RETAINING WALLS

Use retaining walls to create raised beds for planting material or to support a paved terrace area.

- At the correct height, a retaining wall makes excellent casual seating when entertaining friends outdoors.
- Retaining walls are particularly attractive when trailing plants are chosen to grow over them.
- If designed carefully, raised flower beds can make garden maintenance practicable for the elderly, because they make planting more accessible.

△ RAISED BED
This handsome, formally planted, retaining wall is a charming feature in itself against the backdrop of hedging.

27 TRAILING PLANTS

Choose plants with a trailing habit to break up and soften the lines of a retaining wall or any other vertical structure, such as a balcony rail.

- Nasturtiums, *Tropaeolum*, make particularly attractive trailing plants, with their tumbling form, long-lasting flowers, and shapely leaves.
- Many less invasive climbers, such as Black-eyed Susan (*Thunbergia alata*) are suitable as trailers.

NASTURTIUM

TRAILING PLANT CHOICE
Aubrieta deltoidea
Euonymus fortunei
Genista lydia
Juniperus
Rosmarinus lavandulaceus
Salvia officinalis
Verbena

◁ HANGING GARDEN
An annual verbena spills over the edge of a simple wooden trough.

28 SECONDARY FENCING

Consider using fencing within your garden space as well as around it to create a room-like area for entertaining visitors or for sunbathing – the degree of privacy will depend on your choice of material (*see p.23*).

- Back a garden feature such as a sculpture with screens made from fencing materials.
- Provide support for climbing plants with openwork or simple cane and wire fencing.
- Use a wire fence to keep pets away from your plants without obstructing your view.

△ SIMPLE DIVISION
Here, sweet pea (Lathyrus odoratus) is supported by an improvised fence composed of twigs linked by string.

29 DISGUISES FOR EYESORES

Position fencing, or another screening material, to hide parts of the garden you would rather not see, such as dustbins, a compost heap, or an oil tank. Alternatively, planting can be used to hide unsightly areas, but this course may require patience.

- An openwork fence, such as trellis, supporting a climbing plant makes an attractive screen. But be sure to choose an evergreen plant or the eyesore will be exposed each winter.
- Evergreen hedging plants, such as box, also form very effective screens.

△ DISGUISES WITH IVIES
An ugly drain pipe is partially hidden by a small-leafed variegated ivy. Climbing plants are often ideal for softening ugly walls.

△ SCREENS & GREENS
A simple screen conceals a compost heap in a shady part of the garden. The screen also serves as a backdrop to potted plants.

30 CREATING HIDDEN STORAGE SPACE

If possible, try to include a space for storing items like tools and furniture in your garden design. If there is no space for a small shed, build a cupboard space in a material that suits the style of your house.

- Another solution to the problem of storage space in small gardens is to purchase a tool set with a single detachable handle and a range of compatible tool heads – including hoes, rakes, trowels, and cultivators.

△ ATTRACTIVE TRELLIS
A trellis can disguise an ugly wall – whether it is planted or simply painted.

31 TRELLISWORK FENCING

Use trellis, available in either square- or diamond-patterned designs, to support climbers on a wall or fence. Freestanding trellis is handy for instant partitions and openwork screening.
- Trelliswork can be painted or stained and then attached to a wall as a feature in itself (*see p.61*).
- Extend the height of existing walls without blocking out the light, by adding a trellis fence.
- A glimpse through trellis will, by blurring the outlines of what lies beyond, give the smallest of spaces the illusion of size.

△ STURDY TRELLIS
For planting, make sure that your trellis is strong, and attach it with galvanized nails.

SQUARE-PATTERNED TRELLIS

DIAMOND-PATTERNED TRELLIS

32 PERGOLAS

Pergolas have many practical and visual uses in a small garden:

- A pergola can be used to define a room-like space in semi-shade for eating and entertaining outdoors.
- It can form a sheltered transition between two separate buildings.
- Use a pergola to reinforce the lines of a path or to direct the eye towards an interesting design feature or view.
- Pergolas can be built in a variety of materials to complement the design of your house and garden.
- Draped in climbing plants, a free-standing pergola can be a stunning feature in its own right.

△ **TIMBER PERGOLA**
This attractive timber pergola is supported on one side by brick columns that match the brick patio below.

▽ **STRETCHED WIRE**
Wire stretched by a tensioner forms a taut and discreet pergola horizontal that allows the maximum amount of light to penetrate.

△ **TIMBER SUPPORTS**
Timber is the most common material for pergolas. Softwoods are adequate but must be pressure-treated with a preservative.

SHAPED, PAINTED SOFTWOOD △
These painted horizontals have been cut in decorative shapes. They are supported by scaffolding poles, which are painted white.

33 PLANTS FOR PERGOLAS

Pergolas, whether they are free-standing or adjoining a building, make wonderful hosts to climbing plants. Use plants to soften the overall structure and to provide attractive dappled shade, but bear in mind what the effect will be in winter.

- Plants on pergolas also provide privacy, which can be a great benefit in small urban gardens.
- Remember to consider the weight of planting in relation to the strength of the pergola.

PERFECT FOR PERGOLAS
Actinidia chinensis
Campsis grandiflora
Hedera colchica
Hedera helix 'Hibernica'
Jasminum officinale
Lonicera japonica
Parthenocissus henryana
Polygonum baldschuanicum
Vitis coignetiae
Vitis vinifera
Wisteria

SCENTED ROSES ▷
Fragrant climbing roses can fill a pergola with colour and perfume.

◁ VINE
A grape vine (Vitis vinifera) *will thrive on a pergola in most situations.*

34 POINT OF FOCUS

Strategic focal points in your design will help determine how the eye travels around the garden. The focal point might be a "special" plant or ornamental tree, but you could equally choose a piece of sculpture, a decorative pot, or even a pergola.

- A focal point can serve to lead the eye to an attractive area or distract the eye away from an ugly feature.
- In a small garden it is often best to use a single, dramatic point of focus.

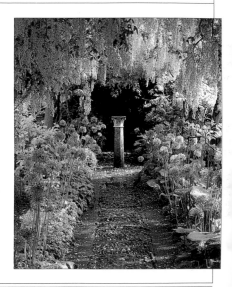

A STRIKING FOCAL POINT ▷
A simple stone pedestal provides a strong focal point at the end of this path, framed by the hanging racemes of a laburnum.

35 CHOOSING SCULPTURE

Take great care when choosing a piece of sculpture or a statue as your choice will have a significant influence on the style and mood of your small garden – adding an elegant finishing touch or an element of humour. Do not, however, be timid with your choice. Generally, the larger the object, the greater the impact it will have. As well as providing a focal point for the garden, it should work from inside the house too. Place your statue in a commanding position, although not necessarily dominating – you may want your sculpture to counterbalance some other feature.

▽ A STATUE FOR REFLECTION
By the waterside, this statue helps to create a contemplative and tranquil atmosphere.

CLASSIC CHOICE ▷
This moss-covered figure, with ivy trained around its base, is ideal for a small formal garden.

△ SCULPTURAL POT
A classical-style urn can be a feature in itself.

36 THE PERFECT POT

The right pot with no planting at all can assume a sculptural quality and demands the same consideration that you would afford to the selection of a piece of sculpture. A classical-style urn, for example, albeit made from reconstituted stone or fibreglass, is grand in style and may not be suited to a location that is humbler in feel. A pot that neither relates to the scale of a space nor the overall style can ruin the total effect.

37 ORNAMENTAL TREES

Ornamental trees provide wonderful living sculptural features, but take account of the eventual height of a tree – one that is too large will quickly engulf and unbalance your design. You may want a tree to give shade and shelter (both for yourself and your plants), but consider also that each tree has its own decorative appeal. A magnolia, for example, bears glorious blossoms; and the maple (*Acer palmatum*) displays colourful autumn foliage.

MAGNOLIA △

△ GLORIOUS COLOUR
Japanese apricot (Prunus mume) *bears spectacular blossoms in early spring.*

BRIGHT FOLIAGE ▷
*Robinia pseudoacacia
'Frisia' is popular for its
striking golden foliage.*

38 TIPS FOR TOPIARY

Topiary (training and pruning shrubs to produce bold artificial shapes) can be used to great effect in a small formal garden. In an informal garden, too, a sculptured plant can act as a foil for unruly planting.

- Simple geometric shapes suit small spaces better than figurative designs.
- Where topiary plants are adjacent to buildings, try echoing the shape of an architectural feature, such as an arch.

△ TRAINING IVY
ON A FRAME

◁ CLIPPED
BOX SPIRAL

39 FURNITURE FEATURES

In a small garden, it is particularly important that any furniture should be an integral part of your whole design rather than an afterthought.

- Be aware of how the style of your furniture suits that of your garden.
- Consider the impact of the shape and colour of your furniture.
- Take as much care positioning your furniture as you would with a mass of planting or a piece of sculpture.

△ FOCAL POINT
A path leads the eye as well as the feet to this eye-catching piece of furniture, helping to make it into a sculptural feature in itself.

◁ ELEGANT IRON
This elegant but weathered wrought-iron seat would be an ideal piece of furniture for a country-style garden (see p.64).

40 WATER FEATURES

When used sympathetically, even a small area of water is always eye-catching, even mesmerizing, when sunlight plays on its surface.

■ The sound of water trickling or flowing gently can be relaxing, and can help to neutralize urban noise.

■ Even where there is little ground space, water can be included in the garden in the form of a wall spout.

■ As a general rule, the simpler the use of water in a small garden, the more effective it will be.

SIMPLE WATER FEATURE

41 PLANTING IN & AROUND WATER

Even the most humble water feature can be enhanced by suitable planting both in and around it. Do not, however, attempt to recreate a natural pond look in a small garden, for this leads to a rather contrived and self-conscious appearance. The smaller the quantity of water, the more restrained both the number and variety of plants should be. Use the vertical stems of irises to contrast with the horizontal line of the water surface, or to counterbalance water pouring from a spout.

WATER PLANTS
Aponogeton distachyos
Eichhornia crassipes
Hydrocharis morsus-ranae
Nymphaea candidissima
Nymphoides peltata

MARGINAL PLANTS
Hemerocallis
Hosta
Iris kaempferi
Lysichiton americanus
Peltiphyllum peltatum
Primula florindae

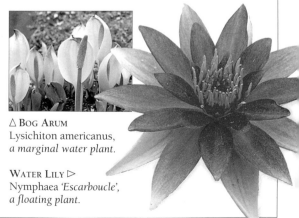

△ BOG ARUM
Lysichiton americanus, *a marginal water plant.*

WATER LILY ▷
Nymphaea *'Escarboucle', a floating plant.*

42 PLANNING A SMALL ROCKERY

Rockeries can make lovely features, but be sure to make your rockery as authentic as possible – an imitation of an alpine rock outcrop as opposed to a pile of discarded rubble in a builder's yard. Select natural rock rather than concrete, and take care to keep any natural veins and crevices flowing in the same direction. Alpine plants, such as gentians and spring crocus, are adapted for specialized climatic conditions and so require excellent drainage and bright light to thrive. If your soil is heavy, dig out the proposed site of your rock garden and replace the soil with a layer of rubble, stone, or ash.

△ ROCK PLANTING
Aubrieta and saxifrage will thrive in a well-prepared rock garden.

EXPOSED SITES ▷
Heathers, grasses, and low-growing rock plants are ideal for exposed sites.

43 SWIMMING POOLS & JACUZZIS

A lap pool – designed for the sole purpose of swimming laps – need not be more than 3 m (10 ft) in width, but should be no shorter than 7 m (23 ft) long. It is therefore possible to fit a lap pool in a small garden, though little room will be left for anything else. A plunge pool is a smaller alternative. When fitted with a wave machine it can provide a force of water against which to swim. If exercise is not a priority, jacuzzis are smaller still. Whatever design you choose, you must cover an outdoor heated pool to conserve energy, so keep the shape simple.

44 PLAY AREAS

With a little effort, a garden can be made into a child's paradise:

Sand-pit and nearby slide

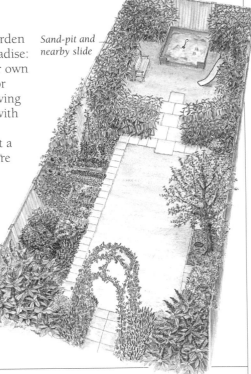

- Children enjoy tending their own gardens, so leave a small plot for your child to plant quick-growing annuals, such as sunflowers, with suitable miniature tools.
- Trees may be able to support a swing – even if this is just a tyre secured to a length of rope.
- When building a play area, keep in mind an alternative use for later years. A raised sand-pit, for instance, could be turned into a pond.
- Avoid plants with thorns or poisonous berries.

A CHILD'S PARADISE ▷
This garden, designed with children in mind, has been planted with species, such as Buddleia, that attract butterflies.

TRADITIONAL BIRD-BATH

45 ATTRACTING BIRDS

Stone bird-baths (traditional features in many formal- and cottage-style gardens) can provide a delightful focal point in a small garden, regardless of whether you are interested in attracting wildlife. If you *are* a keen bird-spotter, consider growing plants that attract birds. Where space permits, an apple tree is possibly the best choice. It supports a host of insects, which birds will feed on; its blossoms are enjoyed by bullfinches; and a wide variety of birds will be enticed by its fruit. However small your garden, there will always be space for a simple bird-table, a nesting box, or a nut-basket.

CONSIDERING SURFACES

GRAVEL & TILE

46 SUITABLE SURFACES

The surface material you choose for your outside space should suit your garden as much as the flooring inside your home suits its various rooms. Give serious consideration to the colour, style, cost, and practical suitability of the various options that are available to you. Materials can be successfully mixed, but always be sure of the final result that you want to achieve.

47 HARD OR SOFT SURFACES?

Hard surfaces such as stone and concrete provide ideal hard-standing for furniture, pots, and other features. They require minimal maintenance, and hard paving can be a feature in its own right.

Gravel and other soft materials are ideal for laying in locations where little will grow and where paving is impractical, such as beneath a tree. The best solution is often a balance of both hard and soft surfacing that creates interesting textural patterns.

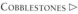

COBBLESTONES ▷
An attractive traditional material, cobbles are not the most comfortable of surfaces to walk on.

◁ GRAVEL & WOODCHIPS
Soft surfaces come in a huge variety of textures and colours and are easy to lay in awkward areas.

48 PAVING PATTERNS

Small pavers are ideal for creating surface patterns. Traditional brick pavers can be used to create a variety of different effects. Set them in a basket-weave pattern, for example, to create a cottage-like, country flavour; interlocking boxes create a strong graphic effect; and a herringbone pattern gives a more random informal look.

△ RADIAL DESIGN
Small unit paving has been used in this garden to create an interesting radial design that is softened by planting.

BASKET WEAVE

INTERLOCKING

HERRINGBONE

49 PAVING CHOICE

When selecting paving, opt for a colour to blend with your house. Wet it before you buy as you want it to look good in all weather. The colour of paving can change dramatically in the rain, and some surfaces can become very slippery.

- It is all too easy to settle for what your local stockist holds, the range of materials generally available is now extremely varied, so try to shop around.

△ TEXTURED PAVING
Textured slabs provide an inexpensive and convenient alternative to small units.

▽▷ SMALL UNIT PAVING
Small pavers create a richly textured look and make paving awkward areas relatively easy. But they are more expensive to lay than larger paving slabs.

△ INTERLOCKING PAVERS

▽ NATURAL STONE
Its variable thickness makes natural stone difficult to lay, but it is always attractive.

△ TERRACOTTA

△ GRANITE PAVERS

50 THE BENEFITS OF GRAVEL SURFACES

Gravel or shingle is suitable for just about any location in the garden.
- Gravel is cheaper and easier to lay than hard surfacing materials such as concrete, stone, and brickwork.
- Many plants will grow through gravel if it is not more than 10 cm (4 in) in depth. Planting in areas of gravel rather than in specific beds of soil creates a random, relaxed look.
- Gravel is useful for brightening up a dank area such as a basement, or for surfacing a flat rooftop.

△ A HARMONIOUS SETTING
Gravel chips of the same stone used in the wall and edgings provides a harmonious setting for the planting in this garden.

STONE-TYPE GRAVEL

FINE COLOURED GRAVEL

SHINGLE

△ GRAVEL PATH
Replenish the top layer of gravel each summer to keep it looking neat and crisp.

51 CHOOSING & USING GRAVEL

A wide range of gravel is available, so be sure to select a variety that suits your home. For driveways, it is wise to choose larger chippings that will not be trapped in the treads of your car tyres. Areas of gravel or shingle must always be properly contained (usually by edging tiles) to prevent chips spreading onto nearby beds and lawns. Rake the surface at regular intervals if you do not want plants to self-seed through the gravel. Although gravel is noisy to walk on, this can serve as a deterrent to intruders.

52 WOOD SURFACING

Decking is especially useful for creating a level outdoor space if your garden slopes dramatically. It also makes an attractive surface in its own right, and has long been popular in the United States, where many houses are built from wood.

- In damp conditions, decking often becomes slippery. Tack a coarse gauge chicken wire to the decking surface to solve this.

△ DECKING PATHWAY
Here, a linear decking path is interrupted by a static circular design. Decking can be used as an alternative to paving, and gives a unified look when combined with fencing.

DECKING PATTERNS

53 SMALL LAWNS

Lawns can be beautiful to look at, but even the smallest lawn will require a considerable amount of work if it is to remain attractive. If you have children and pets, be sure to choose a hard-wearing grass for your area of lawn. For small areas taking no wear, consider using chamomile or low-growing thymes as planting for your lawn.

◁ A TIDY LAWN
A well-maintained lawn is a delight to look at, and makes a good place for the family to relax in the summer sunshine.

54 GROUND COVER

In a small garden, ground-cover plants make an excellent alternative to grass, especially in awkward-shaped areas. They can be used to link taller plants within a mixed planting scheme, or on their own to contrast with hard surfaces or gravel. For year-round cover choose an evergreen, such as ground ivy (*Glechoma hederacea*).

■ Ground-cover plants are ideal for suppressing weeds. However, be sure to contain those plants described as rampant or invasive or you may be forced to spend as much time keeping them under control as you would spend pulling up weeds.

GROUND IVY
Glechoma hederacea *is an evergreen, which provides year-round ground cover.*

GROUND-COVER CHOICE
Ajuga reptans
Anthemis cupaniana
Armeria maritima
Caltha palustris
Euonymus fortunei
Festuca glauca
Lamium maculatum
Lavandula
Polygonum bistorta
Saponaria ocymoides
Stachys lanata
Thymus

GROUND-COVER PLANTING DESIGN
In this garden design, ground-cover plants provide year-round interest with flower colour, texture and leaf-shape.

Stepping stones help keep plant masses separate and allow access for gardener

This creeping rose, Rosa 'Nozomi', has pink and white flowers

Old-fashioned pinks, Dianthus, have masses of fragrant flowers

Lamb's ears (Stachys lanata) has charming, woolly grey foliage

PLANNING YOUR PLANTING

STRUCTURED DESIGN

55 STRUCTURAL PLANTING

Once the hard structure of your garden is in place, bring it to life with planting. For a harmonious effect in a small garden, it is crucial to consider your planting as a whole.
■ Choose planting material that is in scale with the layout and features of your garden.
■ Consider the composition of each grouping of plants; plant in masses rather than singles.
■ Opt for distinctive shapes, forms, textures, or fragrances to provide year-round interest.

56 FEATURE PLANTS

When planning your garden, first decide what your feature plants, or "specials", are going to be. These can be used as a visual link between your planting and the surrounding architecture, for instance a weeping cherry, *Prunus*, curving over a pool wall. On a much smaller scale, your "special" planting might be a yucca acting as an evergreen pivot among a group of perennials.

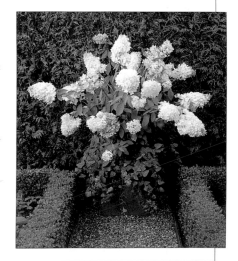

DECIDUOUS FEATURE PLANT ▷
This hydrangea provides a glorious focal point. By using a pot, you can easily swap feature plants when they are past their best.

57 SKELETON PLANTS

Once you have chosen your feature plants, select species that will establish the year-round structure of your garden. As a guideline, go for plants that look good in winter: evergreen plants that will be eclipsed in summer by attention-seeking shrubs, but which come into their own in winter either for their form or foliage. Ivy is particularly useful for small gardens, as are euonymus, cotoneasters, and mahonias. Grow bay and box as clipped container subjects. Within borders, smaller evergreens and shrubby herbs such as hebes can be used as a backbone.

△ SPRING
The clipped box acts as a backdrop to the lime-green flowerheads of euphorbia.

△ SUMMER
In summer the euphorbia changes colour and many annuals appear.

△ AUTUMN
The euphorbias are now dead-headed, Michaelmas daisies provide the colour.

58 SEASONAL INTEREST

Having selected your skeleton plants, choose your seasonal decorative shrubs. In small gardens, shrubs that perform well over two or three seasons provide the best value. Group shrubs to keep them in scale with the design of your garden; the width of the terrace they border, for instance. Avoid using too many single specimens as they may compete with the feature plants.

◁ A SEASONAL SPRAY
This helictotrichon produces a spray of flowers from May to June, when it is engulfed in white dianthus and foxgloves.

59 PLANTING PRETTIES

Once the framework of your planting has been established then choose annuals and biennials to fill in any gaps while you wait for your long-term planting to become established. Annuals can be found in an enormous variety of colours and habits, so select your plants carefully to suit the site and colour scheme. Sunflowers, for example, are annuals that grow to over 3 m (10 ft) tall, making ideal infillers at the back of a sunny border. Fast-growing climbers such as hop can fulfil the same function. For quick infillers at a lower level, you might choose pot marigolds, nasturtiums, or forget-me-nots.

△ COMBINED COLOUR
Campanulas, and orange rock roses, Helianthemum, *combine well.*

▽ ANNUAL BORDER
Annuals grow in a vast range of colours and forms; a species can be found to fill any part of a border.

SEASONAL INFILL ▷
A species of pansy, Viola, *can be found to come into flower in every season, so they are excellent infillers.*

60 THE BEAUTY OF BULBS

Bulbous plants are particularly useful in a small garden because they can be lifted out of the ground after their flowering period and stored away until the following year – allowing space for other infillers to take their place. Bulbs are ideal for windowboxes as they can be planted in layers below other plants, making the most of the limited space. Their upright form provides a pleasing contrast to trailing plants. Many bulbs, such as the narcissus shown here, are ideal for cutting, and a vase of cut flowers taken from the garden is an ideal way of creating a link between inside and out (*see p.10*).

△ NARCISSUS
'GRAND SOLEIL D'OR'

▽ CONTRASTING MASSES
Spring-flowering bulbs, such as these yellow lily-flowered tulips and violet muscari, are ideal for planting en masse.

61 COLOUR IN YOUR GARDEN

Choose plants that combine to create a harmonious colour composition, as opposed to a strongly contrasting one, to give your garden a sense of unity, and, as a result, a greater sense of space. Be aware of the effect colour has on the mood of your garden.

- Yellow and gold are warm, sunny colours that will brighten any area.
- Varying shades of purple combine well with deep greens and bronzes to provide a sombre, mysterious air.
- Choose plants with grey and silver foliage to create a light, airy feel.

△ A MEDLEY OF HUES
Cottage gardens are characterized by their random mixtures of colour. Note how reds dominate other colours.

62 SCENTED GARDEN

Small gardens really come into their own when planted for fragrance. The smaller your space, the closer to your scented plants you will be; the more enclosed your space, the more intense their perfume. To enjoy the scent of flowers, both outside and in your home, plant fragrant roses around your windows and aromatic herbs in a tub by your kitchen door. Grow fragrant lilies and hyacinths in containers on the patio, or cut them and fill your home with perfume.

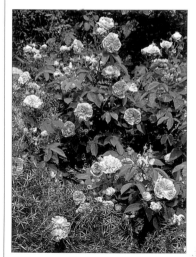

△ HEAVENLY SCENT
Damask roses have a heady fragrance. These old-fashioned roses are popular favourites for country-style gardens.

◁ SCENTED SHRUB
Viburnum x burkwoodii
has sweet-scented flowers.

PLANTING ENVIRONMENTS

63 ANALYZING YOUR ENVIRONMENT

Assess your site so you are aware which areas of the garden are most suitable for which species of plants. How well, if at all, plants thrive in your garden will depend on a number of factors:

■ How much sun reaches your site? Note the direction of the sun at noon in relation to your house, and observe also where shade is cast by boundary fences, trees, and so on.

■ Winds and draughts can render a garden unusable, so check which direction winds are coming from.

■ Analyze your soil. Is it an acid or an alkaline soil? Is it waterlogged or dry? These factors will dictate which plants will grow successfully.

SITE ASSESSMENT ▷
This garden is exposed to sun for long periods but the solid fence gives an area of shade.

Hardy rose tolerates draughty site

Ivy grows up shady wall

Container plants grown on patio area

Raised bed for rock plants

64 SUN-LOVING PLANTS

Most plants love sunshine, and the real sun-lovers – snapdragons, dahlias, geraniums, and gladioli, to mention but a handful – produce the most strikingly colourful flowers. Half-hardy plants, the majority of fruits, and roses all thrive in full sun. For areas of intense sunshine that are prone to droughts, cacti and succulents, palms, and yuccas will survive even baking conditions. Generally, look for species that are naturally conditioned for survival in hot, sunny climates. Most Mediterranean plants are ideal.

△ DAHLIA

△ MORNING GLORY
A fast-growing annual, Convolvulus tricolor *'Blue Flash' displays its intense blue flowers in summer.*

PLANTS THAT THRIVE IN FULL SUNSHINE

Agapanthus	Geranium	Rosmarinus
Buddleia davidii	Hebe	Salvia
Cistus	Iris germanica	Stachys lanata
Cortaderia	Lavandula	Tamarix hispida
Dianthus	Papaver orientale	Viola hederacea

65 SEMI-SHADE PLANTS

Although the majority of plants require the maximum amount of light to achieve their optimum growth, not all plants will tolerate strong direct sunlight, and many species prefer to grow in a shaded area. Plants that enjoy light shade include the fragrant honeysuckle and the ever-popular fuchsia. In general, look for plants that are naturally acclimatized to woodland conditions, such as hydrangeas, lilies, and azaleas.

△ HONEYSUCKLE
An attractive and fragrant climbing plant, honeysuckle brings perfume and colour to shady locations.

PLANTS THAT THRIVE IN SEMI-SHADE

Aucuba	Helleborus	Nicotiana
Bergenia	Impatiens	Polygonum
Buxus	Lilium	Skimmia
Convallaria	Muscari	Vinca
Cyclamen	Myosotis	Viola

66 DRY SHADE PLANTING

Many plants that enjoy sunshine will nevertheless tolerate shady conditions if the soil remains suitably dry. These plants, which include many colourful species, such as *Liriope muscari*, can do much to brighten dull sites. However, the majority of plants that actually enjoy shady conditions are usually chosen for the texture, shape, or sheen of their foliage.

△ LILY TURF
Liriope muscari is an evergreen perennial that will tolerate dry shade. Its spikes of lavender flowers appear in the autumn.

PLANTS SUITABLE FOR DRY SHADE

Ajuga	Lamium	Ruscus aculeatus
Bergenia	Lonicera pileata	Sambucus
Cotoneaster	Lunaria	Skimmia japonica
Cyclamen coum	Osmanthus	Tellima
Hedera helix	Polygonatum	Vinca major
Ilex	Pulmonaria	Viola labradorica

67 DAMP SHADE PLANTING

Some of the hardier species of plant that ideally prefer sunshine will nevertheless tolerate shady conditions as long as soil is sufficiently moist. Willow Gentian, *Gentiana asclepiadea*, is a perennial with sprays of rich-blue, late-summer flowers that can bring colour to a damp shady area. Other favourites for damp shady conditions include marsh marigold, *Caltha palustris*; toad lily, *Tricyrtis formosana*; wake robin, *Trillium grandiflorum*; and *Jeffersonia dubia*.

WILLOW GENTIAN

PLANTS SUITABLE FOR DAMP SHADE

Aruncus dioicus	Hamamelis	Lythrum
Astilbe	Hedera colchica	Pieris
Aucuba japonica	Helleborus	Rheum palmatum
Camellia	Hosta	Sambucus
Cornus	Hydrangea	Viburnum davidii
Fatsia japonica	Ligustrum	Viburnum opulus

68 EXPOSED SITES

Grow tough shrubs, such as berberis, to shelter less hardy plants in exposed areas. If this is not possible, look for resilient plants, such as African daisy (*Osteospermum jucundum*). Tough grasses and heathers can be combined effectively, their massed forms provide a sculptural quality. Low-growing herbs, such as thyme, are hardy plants; succulents, such as houseleek, are useful for ground cover in exposed sites; and strap-leaved plants such as yuccas will also grow successfully. As a guide, look for plants that grow naturally in coastal areas, where winds are particularly punishing.

EXPOSED SITE CHOICE
Berberis
Centranthus ruber
Cistus
Cytisus
Daphne
Erica
Gaultheria procumbens
Genista lydia
Juniperus horizontalis
Lavandula
Philadelphus
Rosmarinus
Spartium junceum
Syringa patula
Ulex europaeus
Viburnum davidii

◁ AFRICAN DAISY

△ ANTHEMIS
A resilient and attractive, evergreen, carpet-forming species, Anthemis punctata *bears a mass of daisy flowers in early summer.*

△ SEA HOLLY
An upright plant adapted to harsh coastal conditions, Eryngium x oliverianum *bears striking lavender-blue flowers.*

POTS &
CONTAINERS

69 PRACTICAL POTS

Containers really come into their own in the small-space garden, as they make it possible to grow plants of any size in almost any location. They provide a practical way of decorating roofs, walls, decks, balconies, basements, and windows as well as the more usual ground levels.

▪ Position pots to punctuate the layout of your small garden, and as a means of introducing planting into any confined or awkward spaces.

POTTED ROSE
Pots can bring colour and fragrance to paved areas of your small garden.

70 POTS OF STYLE

Choose pots carefully. Think about how the colour, shape, and scale of your container will relate to the style and scale of your space.
▪ Half barrels, found at many garden centres, suit most situations.

▪ Terracotta containers should be frost-proof, and simple in outline.
▪ Baskets make excellent short-term containers, when lined with plastic, and look charming when they are filled with sun-loving flowers.

◁ STUDIO POTS

BASKETS, PLAIN ▷
WILLOW OR PAINTED

▽ WOODEN
BARREL

71 USING POTS WITHOUT PLANTING

When choosing a container, ask yourself whether you want the pot, trough, or tub to be the main focal point rather than the plants.

A lovely oil jar, for instance, can be used without planting, providing pleasure in its shape and its contrast to the froth of surrounding plants.

72 PLANTS IN POTS

Just about any type of plant – be it a herb, a vegetable, or a small tree – can be grown in container, provided it is given sufficient root space and is adequately watered and fed.

- Select a pot that complements the planting grown in it. As a rule of thumb, a plant should never be more than twice as tall as its pot.
- Consider colour harmony – do you want a dramatic contrast or a subtle combination.
- Revitalize your established potted plants by replacing the top layer of compost each spring.

STANDARD CHRYSANTHEMUM ▷
Plants grown as standards, such as this chrysanthemum, look particularly attractive when grown in pots. The trailing plant at its base is Stonecrop, Sedum.

△ STRAWBERRY POT
PLANTED WITH HERBS

73 POTTED HERBS

All shrubby herbs make good container plants. Place a pot of mixed herbs next to your kitchen door or beneath the window – as well as being convenient for culinary use, it will also be decorative and pleasantly fragrant.

- A strawberry pot is suitable for planting a mixture of herbs. Flowering chives, *Allium*, winter savoury (*Satureja montana*), and shrubby thymes, *Thymus*, are useful decorative herbs.
- Larger plants such as bay are particularly attractive grown as single specimens in pots.
- Mint should always be potted, as it is invasive.

74 POTTED TREES

A tree planted in a container will provide long-term sculptural interest in your small garden. Where space permits, display tender trees, such as *Citrus* spp. (which can make ideal container plants), on the patio in summer and bring them indoors over the winter months.

- Trees that are grown in pots will limit the height and spread of their growth to compensate for the confined root space.
- Revitalize your potted tree by replacing the top layer of compost each spring, and repot completely every three to five years.

△ LEMON TREE
A Lemon tree grown in a pot makes a stylish feature for a patio space in a Mediterranean-style garden.

75 ARRANGING POTS

Groups of containers may not be significant in a larger garden, but they can be very effective in a smaller garden or on roof terraces, decks, and balconies. But take care when arranging your pots – a jumble of pots can look charming in the right environment, but a jumble can easily become a mess.

- Create a sense of decorative unity by arranging a group of similar pots, related in style and/or colour.
- With informal arrangements, the choice of plants should be formal enough to avoid the overall effect looking too messy.

▽ STYLISH ARRANGEMENT
Grow plants in pots of a similar style to emphasize the plants' foliage and flowers.

76 USING CONTAINERS IN EXPOSED SITES

Plastic containers are useful for exposed sites such as rooftops and balconies. They are lighter than the natural materials they so often imitate and they retain moisture.

A layer of pea gravel or pebbles on top of the compost will help retain moisture and prevent the soil from drying up and blowing away. It can also look attractive and deter weeds

77 IMPROVISED POTS

Almost any kind of container possessing adequate drainage holes can be used for planting. In the Mediterranean and in Mexico all sorts of cans, pots, and pans are colourfully planted and massed together, bringing colour and interest to doorways, alleyways, and courtyards. There is plenty of scope for inventive use of chimney pots, tea pots, old watering cans and wheel barrows, plastic food containers, and sinks.

◁ CHIMNEY POTS FOR PLANTING
Old chimney pots have become so popular as improvised containers that they are now built in ceramic materials and sold in garden centres expressly for planting.

78 HANGING BASKETS

A hanging basket creates a charming miniature garden in itself that comes into its own when the only outdoor space available is a wall or a doorway. When choosing plants for hanging baskets, or any containers positioned high on a wall, select plants that look good when seen from below or from the side. Most suitable are those whose stems meander gracefully, such as *Ballota* spp., or arch elegantly, such as Boston fern (*Nephrolepis exaltata*).
■ Line your hanging baskets with moss, or a man-made porous material, and use a good-quality compost that will retain moisture.

GOLD COLOUR SCHEME

FURNISHING FACTS

79 LIGHTING

Extend the enjoyment of your small garden by including some form of lighting in your design. It will enable you to read, eat, or simply potter about outside on warm spring and autumn evenings. If you can see your garden from indoors, it will enable you to enjoy a night-time view of it all year round. Use spotlights to illuminate a statue or a group of pots, a courtesy lamp by your door to welcome guests, or a dazzling security light to deter unwelcome visitors.

△ ATMOSPHERIC LIGHTING
Subtle lighting creates a gentle glow beneath a specimen tree.

◁ LOW LIGHTING
Bollards provide ideal low-level illumination in gardens.

80 AWNINGS & FABRIC

Give your garden a sense of luxury by furnishing it with colourful covers, cushions, and umbrellas that will compensate for a lack of planting and create an inviting room-like ambience. Consider using an awning to create a ceiling for your "room". It can provide shade, or conceal a grey sky. It provides privacy if your garden is overlooked by neighbours.

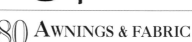

◁ COLOURFUL FABRICS
Fabrics for outside should be tough (and preferably washable) and suit the style of your garden space.

81 DUAL-PURPOSE FURNITURE

Build in furniture to avoid the clutter often created by free-standing chairs and tables (and the problem of storing them in winter). Modify existing features to make seating space, or design new ones so that they serve a dual purpose.

Raise a wall around an existing pool, for example, to provide an area on which to sit, or build retaining walls at a suitable height for casual seating. Use a raised brick or concrete slab as a low table, or build a hollow brick bench for extra storage space.

TIMBER BENCH WITH LIFT-UP LID FOR STORAGE

82 INTEGRATE YOUR FURNISHINGS

Construct built-in furniture from a material that blends in with the rest of your garden. This gives your small garden a unified look that makes it appear larger. If using timber, always choose a hardwood, because softwoods tend to splinter.

Concrete is cheap and durable, but austere. Soften its appearance with trailing plants, or by combining it with another material such as wood. Brick is one of the best materials – its small-unit size makes it possible to build furniture in awkward sites.

83 FREE-STANDING FURNITURE

When space is limited you must take furniture into account from the planning stage onwards. Even the smallest free-standing table with a chair on either side needs a minimum 2 m (6 ft) of clear space – a considerable amount in a small site. Outdoor furniture should not give the appearance of ill-considered clutter; its style must reflect that of the house and garden.

- Permanent furniture should have a settled look, and a bulk that is in scale with surroundings. Often the most satisfactory way of achieving this is by having built-in furniture.
- Make sure that a terrace where furniture is arranged temporarily for summer does not look neglected in winter. Try to visualize how your garden space will look without, as well as with, furniture.

EATING OUT ▷
This well-designed picnic table is sturdy, but many lightweight versions will not stand regular use.

STOWAWAY FURNITURE ▷
Ideal when storage space is limited, this style of furniture is designed to fold flat.

◁ STYLISH FURNISHING
Elegant, wrought-iron furniture such as this is perhaps best suited to a more formal-style garden.

84 TAKING ADVANTAGE OF TREES

Trees usually occupy rather high proportions of space in a small garden. Take maximum advantage of them by using them to save space at ground level. Trees make effective supports for hammocks or swings, for example. They also make ideal supports for lighting, which will illuminate the tracery of branches. Trees provide shade during hot weather, so the base of a tree is the perfect spot for an attractive bench.

UNDER THE APPLE TREE
A white-painted timber bench makes a practical and attractive feature.

85 CO-ORDINATING STYLES

It is worth investing in a beautifully designed and constructed table or chair to link the interior and exterior of your house. The visual connection between the indoor and outdoor space is particularly important with small sites (*see p.10*).

Soften the division between inside and out by having outdoor furniture that complements the style of your indoor furniture, or by linking the the colour of the upholstery. Arrange your outdoor furniture so that it looks good from indoors too.

ILLUSIONS OF GRANDEUR

86 THINKING BIG

Avoid cluttering your garden space with a collection of miniature objects. As the art of the interior decorator shows, the fewer the number of objects in a small room, and the simpler the range of colours and fabrics, the larger it will appear. Apply these principles to your outdoor space to create the same effect. Limit the number of objects in your garden, and scale them up, rather than down. Try to stick to a simple range of materials, matching existing structures.

ONE FOR THE POT ▷
The dramatic shape of a single terracotta pot is usually preferable to the clutter that is created by a collection of small pots.

87 TROMPE L'OEIL EFFECTS

There are a number of design tricks and techniques that can be exploited to decorate your garden in a theatrical or dramatic way using paint, trellis, mirrors, or light. These devices can often create the illusion of size in the smallest of areas. Such techniques, referred to collectively as *trompe l'oeil* effects are especially compatible with the style of man-made surroundings and can provide inventive ways of decorating damp, shady spaces where conditions are too inhospitable for plants to grow.

88 DECEPTIVE PERSPECTIVE

Exploit the effect of natural perspective – where distant objects appear to be smaller than nearby objects of the same size – to give your garden the illusion of length.

- Site tall plants in the foreground, and grade down to shorter ones towards the end of the garden.

- Achieve the same effect with pots, which, ideally, should be identical in every way apart from their size.
- Make paths taper as they extend down the length of your garden.
- Grade a boundary fence or hedge so that it gradually shortens towards the end of your garden.

Here, all four trees are the same height

UP THE GARDEN PATH
Although these plots are the same size, the one on the right seems longer due to distorted perspective.

Shortest trees at end of site

Large pot placed in foreground

89 TRELLISWORK TRICKERY

Even if your only outlook is a wall, you can still create spectacular effects and spatial illusions using trelliswork designs to manipulate the natural laws of perspective (*see above*). Try painting the wall behind the trellis in a pale recessive colour to emphasize the sense of depth (sky blue and other pale colours will give the impression of distance, while bright red and other bold colours appear to leap forwards towards the viewer).

AN ILLUSION OF SPACE ▷
The design of this trelliswork gives the illusion of depth on a flat surface. Note how some of the batons are tapered.

90 PAINTED ILLUSIONS

An abstract mural or painted *trompe l'oeil* can bring vitality to the dingiest of walls.

- Paint a doorway to suggest another garden lying beyond your own, or a window with a window-box (the window-box could be real).
- Paint plants where the real thing cannot grow or to "thicken-out" the existing vegetation.
- Use exterior grade paint on your garden wall. Different effects can be achieved using matt or eggshell finishes or perhaps by using bold stencils and spray paint to create patterns.
- If paint is your medium you can afford to be bold in your design, because mistakes can be painted over and a fresh start can be made.

△ PAINTED PIGEONS
A charming illusion like this can be created in the smallest and dingiest of locations.

91 MAGICAL MIRRORS

Strategically positioned mirrors will reflect the space that you already have and effectively double the size of your garden visually.

- A mirror placed in a doorway, or a bricked-up archway, can give the impression of being an entrance to an area of garden beyond your own.
- Use a mirror as a screen to obscure an unwanted view in your garden.
- Large areas of mirror can brighten up shady sites and basement areas.
- Always use mirrors at least 6mm (¼ in) thick, and remember that they must be spotless to be effective.

◁ DOUBLE-TAKE
A huge mirror has been positioned on a wall glimpsed through a decorative archway, giving the illusion of a second arch beyond.

92 A TRICK OF LIGHT & SHADE

In areas where natural light is intense, position plants or strong architectural features where they will cast dramatic shadows on the surrounding surfaces. If the light is not intense enough to produce well defined shadows, paint some. Use a range of tones of the same colour to imitate shadows of varying intensity.

■ Increase the amount of sunlight reaching planting in shady areas by using mirrors or water features to reflect light towards the area. But do not place mirrors in bright positions or reflected light may singe plants.
■ Let more light into your garden by replacing a solid fence with an open one to increase the apparent space.

△ LIGHT FEATURE
A "window" cut in a hedge creates an unusual focal point in this small garden.

◁ NATURAL SHADOW
Pergola horizontals create exciting shadows in this sunny Mediterranean site.

93 WORKING WITH WATER

However shallow, a pool of water will always make your space appear larger than it actually is.
■ Use light-absorbent lining, such as black butyl rubber, to make the surface reflect surroundings.
■ Alternatively, use light-reflecting lining (mirror tiles for example) to

reflect overhanging features, such as a piece of sculpture or some eye-catching plants, and increase the amount of light in your garden.
■ A mirror alongside, to reflect the reflections in water, will increase the visual excitement and give your space the impression of size.

A SUITABLE STYLE

94 COUNTRY-STYLE GARDEN

Understanding the essence of a style is the key to interpreting it in your own small space. The classic cottage-style garden has a homely rural image of roses rambling around a door, rough stone walls or open timber fencing, and abundant planting.

- Choose unsophisticated plants – daisy-like flowers, such as chrysanthemums and asters; pot marigolds; sweet peas; and hollyhocks.
- Natural materials are the obvious choice for garden furniture; use anything and everything for containers. Simple clay pots are suitably unsophisticated.

△ COUNTRY FLOWERS
Old-fashioned flowers such as delphiniums, sweet peas, and alliums still form the essence of the cottage-garden look.

◁ COUNTRY-STYLE COLOUR
The clean lines of a simple terracotta container are a foil to the masses of silvery Artemisia and blue Nepeta mussinii.

95 FORMAL GARDEN

The key to a formal garden style is in symmetry and order, characterized by neatly clipped hedges, elegant statuary, straight paths, and closely mown lawns. Such gardens need regular maintenance, for minor flaws tend to leap out from such precisely balanced design.

■ A carefully chosen point of focus, such as an elegant, unplanted oil jar will strike the right note of sophistication. A formal pool might be included to reflect the overall symmetry.

■ Echo a symmetrical layout with moulded terracotta tubs planted with clipped box.

△ FORMAL FLOWERBEDS
Here, the planting is limited so as not to lessen the impact of the overall design.

96 MODERN GARDEN

Simplicity of line and a strong sense of space are characteristics of the modern-style garden. Function takes precedence, so plunge pools and jacuzzis definitely fit the look.

■ Vegetation should be striking and architectural, so incorporate large-leaved hostas and spiky grasses.

■ Large concrete tubs can help create the modern look – terracotta works when the shapes are clean and bold.

■ Make comfort a top priority when choosing furniture. Modern designs, such as "director's chairs", are a popular option.

■ Choose square tiles to divide up your space geometrically.

LESS IS MORE ▷
Restraint is essential when choosing accessories for your modern-style garden.

Large-leaved hosta

97 COLONIAL STYLE

The essence of a colonial-style garden is homeliness and comfort. Position a hammock or rocking chair on a neat, timber verandah to capture the relaxed, unhurried mood. Rose-covered arbours and box hedging can be used to provide an echo of gracious living, but choose simple materials. Statuary is unpretentious – figures of animals in stone or timber are perfect. White picket fencing has the clean crisp colonial look; paths can be laid with slate or simple wood chippings.

▽ COLONIAL CONTAINERS
White-painted pots planted with herbs suggest a folksy simplicity that is the key to colonial-style gardening.

△ RELAXED PLANTING
Planting is allowed to sprawl against the clapboard walls, but notice the gentle counterpoise of the standard rose.

Avoid pretension or abstraction with statuary

Timber is the natural choice for furniture

98 MEDITERRANEAN-STYLE GARDEN

Vivacious colours are the key to a Mediterranean-style garden. Terracotta and ceramic pots should overflow with cascading flowers in vibrant reds, yellows, oranges, and blues against a backdrop of crisp white walls and spiky yucca plants. Create an area of terrace surfaced with stone or terracotta to provide a place to eat outdoors and entertain guests. Shade, therefore, is also a crucial element, and parasols or awnings – the bigger (and brighter) the better – strike the perfect note. Furniture, too, should be brightly coloured, perhaps café-style. A lemon tree in a terracotta tub or a classical stone or ceramic statue provides the archetypal Mediterranean focal point.

△ DECORATIVE FRUIT
If you do not have the space to grow citrus trees in tubs, display the fruit in colourful bowls.

SUITABLE CERAMICS ▷
Simple terracotta tiles provide the appropriate surfacing material for a Mediterranean garden. Colourful glazed ceramic tiles look good on walls, complementing the natural vibrancy of sea and sky.

Use pebbles for decoration

The ubiquitous terracotta pot is ideal

Mosaic tiles

Yucca plant

99 ORIENTAL GARDEN

When creating an oriental-style garden you should aim to instil a mood of serene and contemplative calm into your design. Bamboo or brushwood is appropriate for fencing. Look for textural detailing when choosing containers.

■ Rocks and mossy stones are important styling details for their solid mass and sculptural shapes.

■ Stained decking and gravel (raked into swirling patterns for maximum authenticity) are suitable surfacing materials for an oriental-style garden.

■ Exploit the natural textures and rough shapes of rocks and driftwood to make seats and other furnishings. Always keep seating low.

△ PRACTICAL PAVING
Stone paving is practical if you do not want a gravel pattern to be disturbed.

▽ SOMBRE COLOURS
A water feature adds to the sense of tranquility. Choose planting for its leaf texture. Colours should be sombre.

100 COURTYARD GARDEN

A courtyard garden is an obvious choice for a small enclosed urban area. Patio surfacing, which typifies a courtyard garden, helps to provide a low-maintenance space that is ideal for practical outdoor living.
- Planting can still be enjoyed in containers and small raised beds. Indeed, plants are essential to soften the hard lines of walls and paving.
- Take advantage of vertical space by planting fragrant climbers, such as honeysuckle. Consider a potted tree to provide an area of shade.

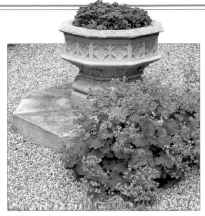

△ FONT FEATURE
An old stone font makes an ideal focal point for this courtyard. Alchemilla mollis *softens the fonts hard lines.*

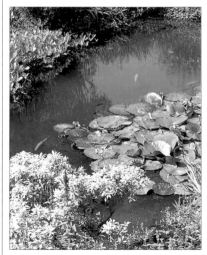

△ INFORMAL POND
This small pond, teeming with golden carp, is ideally suited to its rural setting. Water lilies adorn the surface.

101 WATER GARDEN

Your choice of plant material is crucial when you are planning to establish a small pond.
- The smaller the surface area of the water, the more important it is to include oxygenating plants such as *Elodea canadensis* in your choice.
- Dwarf water lilies, *Nymphaea*, can be planted in water that is only 15 cm (6 in) deep, making them an ideal choice for small ponds.
- Decking is the best surfacing for water gardens; select furniture and fencing in a matching timber. A stone statue will enhance the look.
- Informal ponds can look idyllic in a rural location, but a more formal raised or sunken brick pond is better suited to an urban environment.

INDEX

ACKNOWLEDGMENTS

Dorling Kindersley would like to thank Hilary Bird for compiling the index, Isobel Holland for proof-reading, Murdo Culver for design assistance, and Forest Lodge Garden Centre, Farnham, Surrey for location photography.

Photography

KEY: t *top*; b *bottom*; c *centre*; l *left*; r *right*
All photographs by Geoff Dann and Steve Wooster except;
Peter Anderson 3, 11l, 52t, 53b; Clive Boursell 4; **Boys Syndication** 10l; Linda Burgess (**Garden Picture Library**) 61b; Eric Crichton 50b, 51t; Robert Estall (**Garden Picture Library**) 33br; Neil Fletcher 46t, 49b, 49t; John Glover 62b; Jerry Harpur 51br; Stephen Hayward 66t; Jacqui Hurst 9bl, 13t, 14b, 18l, 20bl, 22l, 22r, 25mr, 28tr, 36l, 45t, 47bl, 65tl; Dave King 10r, 11tr, 11br, 26r, 34mr, 34bl, 58bl, 64tr, 65br, 66b, 67; Andrew Lawson 35br; Andrew de Lory 20tl; Damien Moore 14t, 17t, 19br, 25bl, 127t, 27b, 28br, 31tl, 41tr, 54, 68; Elvin McDonald 13b; Howard Rice 50t; Tim Ridley 5, 23tr, 29, 38t, 41ml, 52b; Kim Taylor 37b; Colin Walton 1, 19t, 42t; Matthew Ward 8, 9tl, 15, 43b, 53t, 55, 72b; **Elizabeth Whiting & Assoc**. 62l.
The designs on pages 8, 9, 15, 53, 55 originally appeared in *Container Gardening* by Malcolm Hillier, Dorling Kindersley, 1991.

Illustrations

Martine Collings 37; Karen Cochrane 39; Liz Peperall 45; Colin Salmon 48